The Darts and the Commentary

Acknowledgements.
Thanks are due to: *Ambit, First Draft, Harry's Hand, Iron, Iron Erotica, Orbis, Poetry and Audience, Radio One, Second Draft, Smiths Knoll, The North, The Rialto, The Wide Skirt, Writing Poems* (Bloodaxe, 1994).

Duncan Curry's pamphlet *Oranges* (now unavailable) was published by Smith/Doorstop Books in 1987.

The Darts and the Commentary

Duncan Curry

Smith/Doorstop Books

Published 1996 by
Smith/Doorstop Books
The Poetry Business
The Studio
Byram Arcade
Westgate
Huddersfield HD1 1ND

ISBN 1 869961 59 5

British Library Cataloguing-in-Publication Data. A catalogue
record for this book is available from the British Library.

Typeset at The Poetry Business
Printed by Peepal Tree, Leeds

Cover by blue door design, Heckmondwike
Cover illustration: 'Jack of Hearts' by Mark Curry

Distributed by Password (Books) Ltd.,
23 New Mount Street, Manchester M4 4DE

The Poetry Business gratefully acknowledges the help of
Kirklees Metropolitan Council and Yorkshire & Humberside
Arts.

CONTENTS

The Darts and the Commentary

but the point is after fifty years
of washing shirts and putting up with sex
and his meanness and endless guff about football
and her mother and paying over the odds for a holiday in Majorca
because she won't go out of season
and hearing again what our Frank's done with his garden
and listening again to that joke she didn't find funny the first time
and putting up with that bloody dog

the point is, caught as both were at nineteen and twenty
she with those tanned Blackpool legs
he with his thirty one and six
'It's a good wage for a young man and it'll only get better'
but it didn't, stuck in the groove of a Jim Reeves' record
on Saturday the dog track, round and round
first born, second, third

and the point *is*, no-one seems to mind.
Albert and Bertha on with their Golden
quietly going home down wet streets
polishing the new car, something worked, something got
to feel good about when next door
lays cursing in the grease and rust and
'Can I borrow your five-eighths?'

A pint at the bar, the latest joke
something snatched, some sort of meaning
taken from the scrape of change in the till drawer
and the quiet thud of double top.
Life's as long as a cigarette
and time is what the landlord calls.
The drape of a towel, that's the point.

Also Ran

And they're off now.
It's Firm Policy, Uncle Max with Mrs Wing Commander.
The first hurdle:
Lunch Box, Mrs Wing Commander, Full of Port.
Hopeful Charmer with Nautical Joke.
And it's Just As Hopeful
with Strong Language and Careless Kiss,
but Mrs Wing Commander is reluctant.
Away We Go, Evening Affair, Uncle Max, The Overnight Man.

Into the second furlong. It's Shy Mistress,
Over and Above, Tom's Whatsisname.
Mrs Wing Commander pushing forward.
It's Brother Patrick. Strong Language,
but Sweet Sarah Jane holds on.
Relatively Easy with Maloney's Daughter.
Uncle Max and French Goblin.

Only three fences to go.
Shy Mistress has the lead,
Brother Patrick coming up behind Cool Jamie,
And here's a surprise:
Mrs Wing Commander goes down!
She's down!
A real tangle there with Senator Snugfit.

And it's Brother Patrick showing Cool Jamie what he's made of.
He's pulling away.
Cool Jamie tries to hold on, but he's losing it.
It's slipping. The gap is widening.
It's neck and neck now.
Brother Patrick, Shy Mistress, Zam-Zam and Tara-Tong.
Final straight – only one furlong to go.
Full of Port, Uncle Max and Shy Mistress,
are giving it all they're worth.

And would you believe it?
It's So Good!
So Good, coming from behind!

He's taking them all.
Strong Language, Brother Patrick and Shy Mistress.
It's So Good!
But Shy Mistress is not to be taken.
She' holding on, she's holding on, yes, yes!
Shy Mistress comes in first,
So Good, Cool Jamie,
a length behind Brother Patrick,
Relatively Easy, Tara-Tong and Zam-Zam.

A Delightful Opportunity to Acquire

There are sycamores and a bowling green
but the end of the road is pot holes.
One hundred and twenty is squeezed between
the chip shop and a railway siding of coal.

The door is difficult over the phone book.
There's a clock card for gas and electric,
a holiday brochure from Thomas Cook
and a postcard to Alison from Nick.

The kitchen 'recently refitted', is small
and the agent's blurb forgets to mention
the bend of gas pipe to the opposite wall
and the stone floor split in two directions.

In the lounge the paper is in heavy bloom;
deep colours shrink the room to half size.
The electric fire has copper flue,
flame effect and smoke which doesn't rise.

The main bedroom is a month of jobs.
A cracked window takes the hill's contour;
wires show from salmon pink plaster, a gob
of paint holds a five litre tin to the floor.

The garden path ends in a tangle
of blackberry bushes and an old fridge.
The fall pipe leans back at an angle
where a slate has pushed to the edge.

I swing the keys as if I owned the place,
go round again and take another look.
In the bathroom, a mirror waits for a face.
I check the back door, nick the phone book.

'Leave it Twenty Minutes to Burn the Newness Off'

(YEB delivery man)

We can smell it a room off:
newness shimmering into clean air.
Rings burning with newness.
Grill aglow with it.

Newness smoking around toast,
skulking under knobs.
Oven boiling with newness.
Cable abuzz with it.

Newness mixing with curry powder,
with cake. 'Have a slice,' you say.
Creamy newness, squidgy in jam.
Apples bubbling in the old pan.

Wooden Buddha

Clutter which I cling to,
as if flotsam will keep me afloat
in this sinking house too heavy with cargo.

Stuffed in the loft, to fall in on me any day
and surprise me with its uselessness:
a wooden statue of a man.

He's always like this: his head in his hands,
never looking up, hunched and holding himself taut
beneath some great weight that presses.

No Sprawl

The lounge is a shop window with carpet
no one walks on. It's difficult as lace.
A row of ornaments, books no-one reads,
a mirror to perfectly reflect space.

Neat is nasty. The colours jump to it –
everything: cactus, cushions, pot pourri.
No-one dare look at the Picasso print,
drop an aitch or sit on the settee.

In the kitchen, the pine hums with wax.
The host serves percolated coffee and mints.
A spotlight shines on an earthenware bowl
of spice bottles – even untidy is meant.

At dawn, in the chosen view,
the cow is fastidious with her tongue,
sheep are careful how they stand
and the horse holds back his dung.

What Do You Bring to This Job?

I'll bring myself in a Fiat 125
because on the money this job pays
I won't be affording anything else
for at least two years.

I'll bring my sandwiches,
though if I crack off with your secretary
I may be able to leave them at home
and go to the pub, lunchtimes.

I'll bring my brown leather briefcase
which served me well in my last job
and will carry around all the bullshit
that you'll be writing.

I'll come wearing a tie, though not
if I'm up late or my cottons need washing.
I'll inspire where inspiration is possible,
but mostly it will be just sweat.

I'll bring a certain wit
to this gormless architecture for twenty eight years
before I shake your golden hand,
heart attack or breakdown not with sitting.

Climbing

Janine is in bedding. She's doing each department.
Did Furnishings last week and sold more
square yards of carpet than the whole floor.

Next, the Outward Bound course in Castleton
(assertiveness training and rock climbing).
Dispatch for a week, Complaints, then Buying.

At the foot of the stairs, her photograph.
Employee of the Month. A high profile.
Hair dark and just right, a confident smile.

A career girl. Says after two years, she's off.
Management are slack, she says, take too long.
Shadows Mr Senior, bites her tongue.

This course is the best, of course, but wants more
than her Datsun and terrace in Penistone.
Something smart where people jump, dress the part.

Bugger Me, It's Do-Dah

Missed her in the first scene –
just a bod in the plot,
the obvious one to run off with the man;
but in the sweeping gardens and the maze high hedges,
she's stealing a drag between duties
and as she turns to kiss the underfootman
I recognise the dark hair under the maid's starched cap.
Told to get on with it by the housekeeper, the scene ends

and I'm in the café talking with her and a friend
about the shell shock of stardom.
Would I swap this comfy seat in the dark
for the flickering image of Herefordshire or wherever it is?
The making of nineteen forty eight is sometimes obvious,
the cars driving past, the Oxo tin in the corner shop.
Her name nags at me for half an hour
so I sit on through the credits.

Waiting

We wait and we wait, but nothing happens.
Only the names are called from time to time:
Edith Green, Nellie Wigley, Margaret Smith.

Someone moves from this room to another,
from a seat in here to a seat in there.
We wait and nothing happens, but we wait.

Alan Brown. A distant call from the depths.
Alan Brown. The name, at last, finds its owner.
Violet Whittaker, Margery Oldroyd.

Only the children are happy,
causing their chaos with new found friends.
Nothing happens, but we wait and we wait.

We get a chance to observe all the staff,
mostly how they walk – brisk and important.
Richard Buttering, Paul White, Wendy Cleeves.

Someone stirs, mistaking the name for hers.
Irritation. Wendy Cleeves. It's eleven-o-clock.
We wait and we wait, but nothing happens.
David Hargreaves, Ian Bould ... Wendy Cleeves.

Osteopath

His conversation is posture, furniture,
the biochemistry of stress. He will flex
your spine laterally, running his palm
down your vertebrae a disc at a time.

He will bend you like a long bow
and knows if the bones will go or not.
He folds you into a special knot
and clicks the combination of your middle back.

He is cruel and kind. The pain bubbles
beneath his fingers and bursts, a sweet agony
which subsides at his touch. Your bones
are an abacus which he sets again to neutral.

Impressed memories are massaged away,
drip through the tears as you dress.
You are fragile in the bright street,
each step new felt through the old structure.

'Is the washing dry yet?'

Five days it's been there.
A blue dress with white collar.
Underpants. Socks. In spring rain,
they get wet. Dry again.

Jeans blown against the bush
like a child swinging upside down on a tree limb.
The grey basket where you left it.
The ringing phone not eased with answering.

September 15th, 1989

The room is a collapsing lung.
I fan you with a towel, red and yellow gill.

We fiddle with sheets, window blinds
small jobs to lend helplessness a purpose.

The ward is quieter now. Across the garden, willow hangs
and a Tree of Heaven burns brown in late sun.

You awaken and all the life left
focuses in your left eye, blue

like a bulb about to break
which grows suddenly brighter.

Firewood

Two by two painted matt black.
I 'squint it up' as you would say. Ill seasoned,
it twists off line. Hardly fit, even for the grave.

I see you shake your head over the slack lid,
chunter about dovetails which show light,
feel the grain and frown: 'Firewood.'

Shortly Before Eleven

I am loading the car with cuttings
when a hearse arrives
and an undertaker looking just like yours
goes quietly to knock.

As I push a rose branch into a bin liner
it looks almost routine –
a coat of polish in October sun,
a Daimler with an open door.

Bicycle

Me, peddling like crazy, protesting that
I'll never stay upright on two wobbling
wheels; behind, running, is you

holding my saddle with your giant's grip,
while trying to steer me, too. We are clowns
without circus or applause.

Suddenly – no reply; encouraging
words are gone: I am balancing alone
down the tightrope of the road.

Any Two

When I look at my father, I can't see him.
He has disappeared in greasy overalls,
wasted years in a divorce he didn't want.

A big beard and glasses over big eyes,
cigarette burning, thousands end to end,
measuring out the miles he drives for work,
the spanners he lifts, the curses he makes,

his trip home in the traffic to an empty house
and no soup on the stove, just three cats,
slinking around uncomfortably,
like his sons who never all got on at once:
'Any two,' he'd say. 'Give me any two.'

Plumbing with my Father

The chance to lean on a spanner saw you proud.
I lit a match and a blowtorch burnt
between us. I saw how the joint had soured:
we were flooded by the tiniest squirt.

Your love is three quarter copper pipe,
shining in the loft. I just had to look.
Your expression is grease, the rag you wipe,
the craftsman's knack not kept in books.

Remote

Harry points and turns me to full:
I'm the neighbours banging on the wall.
He presses me to a whisper:
I mouth the news and weather.

'And next on Two ...' He turns me over:
I'm a thriller before the explosion,
a washing powder excited by whiteness,
a prosecutor urging the witness.

I'm Doctor Charles Webb, level one.
I'm the video channel with nothing on.
He messes with my colour. Picture naff,
aerial askew, he turns me off:

Boys who Throw Stones

I push my finger in and spread the pain.
Dropping a stone into a still pool is the same.
Rings move beyond the water, beyond the wood.
A child falls into adulthood.

I pull my finger out and there is blood.
An idle act, the stone among the mud.
I sit and wait for ripples to die.
When the pond is perfect, I will see the sky.

Swimming

A man came, came when you were seven,
came with his hands and a knowledge,
came when the sun was shining, an ordinary day.
Came and offered you a lift in a car,
came round the corner a little too fast,
kicking up dust on the African road,
came and stopped by your side.
Came to give you a lift to the pool,
you were walking and wanted to be at the pool,
wanted the water on your body.

You came to be there,
no-one at home to take you,
mum and dad busy.
Waited all week, came Friday,
there was only one day left.
Came to it, you'd walk alone.
Came to this point, okay,
the point in the bend,
skipping the straight bit,
the town visible in the valley.
No-one around, only the birds.
No elephants came, no rhino.
Then the car came.

McCoy's Last Stand

Everyone on the back row
is reading, except Brown,
who is fishing for my attention:
he has his book upside down.

He is convincing. He leans forward
and turns a page, backwards.
I see the hook, but today
I am not biting, I am writing.

I imagine the dénouement
in reverse: the hero's bullet
returns to his smoking gun
as the villian's blood spills uphill

and all the deeds are undone
as they eat their words:
'McCoy, surrounded is building whole the
up hands your with out come,'

but McCoy doesn't answer.
He's busy at the bank
handing money to the cashier.
The bell is ringing

School is a Coffee Grinder

School is a coffee grinder and around we go.
Upstairs, management say all day long
what a nice smell and what a good job
they are doing to make such an aroma.

The bells whirl us around and we go,
each obedient bean to our pot.
We write on the importance of coffee
and shout if anyone disagrees.

The beans come in and are ground
and we in turn are ground into granules,
then powder, then the finest dust
which blows away.

Invigilator

He is away, driving the small tractor
with flashing amber light across the pitch,
disembodied in mist,
cutting grass no-one can see to play on,

moving like a blip across a monitor,
the hum of its engine distant,
its headlights briefly visible on the turn,
before moving back down the line,

needing no French to make itself understood,
no verb other than to cut, no raison d'être
other than to work steadily along,
each stroke scanning its territory,

marking out what is his between chalk lines,
owning each piece of ground anew,
at the turn, driving the line back again,
slightly overlapped so no point is lost,

each statement moving to the very edge,
using its time usefully, not squandering itself
in idle discourse or vacant ramblings,
but across and back like a dog pacing its chain.

Thirty Fifteen

The electric fan turns and turns. It is following a fly.
There is absolutely no point to its existence.
It doesn't cool the stifling air, only moves it about.
The room is very big and from here we can't feel it.

Tick goes the clock. Whirr goes the fan. Cough the candidates.
Rustle goes the paper. Shine go the calculators.
The electric fan looks for an answer, shakes its head.
It is high up on a table umpiring a tennis match. It is listening

to an argument: the boy played too much football.
The girl saw too much television.
The fan needs maths: circles, ninety degrees.
It is our stupid friend. Look at him looking.

Visitors' Book

From Folkestone to Ontario,
the names and addresses wriggle
in red ink down the page. I turn
back to nineteen seventy nine,

where Mr and Mrs Lockwood
(in blue) from Devon found the place
'delightful', while Jackie and Ken
from Edinburgh thought it 'ACE!'

Ron Hardcastle from Rotherham
is characteristically terse:
'Too dear!' Underneath his rebuke,
his wife had written 'very nice'.

All this practically writes itself –
the columns require familiar
informations given before
at the boarding house or church –

but the final one, the scribbled
request of the owner to say
how and where you first heard of us
gives everybody a problem.

Chas and Pip (LA) bluster
with something about the tourist board
while Miss Gibbs MA., Dip Phil (Oxon)
has no room and ignores it.

Mr Ratcliffe saw an advert,
so did Alison and Shirley.
Mr and Mrs Hammerton-Boyes
from New South Wales were 'just passing'.

For some, things are not straightforward
and rather than squash the truth
by a phrase or two, they struggle
in the small space to be honest.

Anne, on the school trip from Swansea,
hits upon the answer: 'The bus
driver told us'. Thirty five dittos
acknowledge her brilliance.

Back now in the red, ignoring
the tyranny of pencilled columns,
I add my own name and address:
Ossett under Ontario.

Signing

I am so famous they queue up to see me,
spend thirty pounds on perfume and queue up.
My photographs are stacked before me.
I sign a bold flourish across my breasts.

This one chewing gum brings me a library book.
Sorry, I tell him, I can't sign a library book.
In the spotlight, in the big store, on the big avenue,
in the big city, I have to be careful.

My minders flex behind me. Everyone gets thirty seconds.
A pity. I turn my sweetest smile on him.
Any chance of a kiss, then? he says.
I know exactly how I look when I shake my head.

Window

I listen again to the sound of him
coming through the wall and wonder again
what she does to make him so loud,
lie awake until two and it's all talk.

I look into the lounge when I go past.
She wears his denim jacket and his shirts.
Tonight he rumbles on for a full half hour
before letting go.

When we meet at our cars in the morning,
she smiles. He raises the window and waves.
He put his fist through it once,
the glass tinkling out at midnight.

Football

Promised for July, the earth-movers come
And rip up the football pitch behind our house.
The dust sings in the air, clogs our washing
And films the window ledges.
It gathers a premature gloom in every room.
Almost as thick are the rumours:
A car park, a tennis court, a supermarket.
Everything grows from that first slice of turf.

Deaf to the noise, the drivers pummel the earth
All day and late into the evening.
They figure eights and circle each other
Like mating monsters, until finally
They hum down to a silence which grabs our ears.
Men burnt brown drop from yellow machines
Which are owned by Len Dowson of Scarborough.
Across the cabin door, his name is mud.

They park their caravan under the line
Of sycamores and after fish and chips
Sit joking and smoking. A surly one,
The foreman, comes to our kitchen
Every second day for water. I don't refuse.
In a week, the earth is hilled high, ready
For the lorries which track their own road
As they trundle in from the tiny entrance.

At lunchtime, the lorries take the diggers
At football. The pitch is rather ragged now,
With ear muffs and jerseys for goals,
But imagination scores at Edgehill Road
And the generator roars approval. At half-time
They sit on the trench of the touchline,
Burping beer and laughing loudly
At me gathering in the washing.

August is sodden and the work slow,
But the twenty ninth sees the ground level
And the machines pulling out for home.

The earth is left silent to settle
To its new arrangement under the September frost.
Nothing happens until spring, when the dirt track
Of the lorries is pushed back by grass.
It's been a year now and we're no wiser.

Rules of the Game

Go to any square. Montaigu-de-Quercy.
One rule is clear: men. Their eyes upon you.
Each have their own style: spit on the palm or rub,
knees bend, wrist back, aim and swing,

a small ball first, followed by two heavier ones.
It's good to get close with a roll or throw
and good to whack your opponent, if that's who he is,
from the centre to the edge of play.

You know it's serious when the tape measure comes out.
You know the joke, but not the punchline
and it seems you could watch all afternoon
and not work out who's who or what the score really is,

though it's clearly marked with pegs
in hardboard hanging on the hedge.

Loud in the Corner

Bandit, spoilt brat!
Woooooooooooooo Wooooooooooo.
Plus Nudge! Quick Nudge!
Cash trail! Multiplier!
Bar Bar Bar. You drop your lot.

Chunker, chunker, chunker, chunker, chunker.
Chunker, chunker, chunker, chunker, chunker.
Chunker, chunker, chunker, chunker, chunker.
Chunker, chunker, chunker, chunker, chunker.

I want to take a sledgehammer to your strawberries.

For Entertainment Only

The springed plunger back. I wang the ball
up and around the top. It arcs like a star.
Give me proper scores in tens of thousands
and bells that clang my glory on the backboard.

Give me double flippers with hair trigger,
knocking and jerking the ball out of danger,
the sneaky way it's lost in that dodgy middle ground.
Add-ons for extended play.

P'ting, p'ting. Skill bonus, skill reward,
skill extra for hitting the ace.
A queue builds behind me. P'ting, p'ting.
The springed plunger back. I wang the ball.

D'zing, d'zing, d'zing. Hit those flippers.
That dodgy middle ground. Numbers off the scale.
One hundred thousand katrillions.
Bzap! For entertainment only.

Wordsworth is Picking Daffodils

Wordsworth is picking daffodils.
In frock-coat and cravat,
he marches down the lane,
scooping them up by the handful.

He's clearing the entire banking,
madly pulling and thrusting bunches
at his sister who lays them
carefully in the wheelbarrow.

His hair blows in the wind and he swings
his stick in strict rhythm to his step.
He started a week ago in Grasmere
and already he's in Coniston.

He runs up a mound to pull a single flower
from under an elm, tosses it in himself.
The grocer knows the month by him,
sniffs the air and nods to his wife.

At the end of a hard day's picking,
they heave up the barrow behind the cottage
where the sticky smell of dead heads
rises to the bedroom window.

She makes entries in their weekly accounts.
The figures grow into thousands,
but he will not be cheered.
He stares from his couch at the wall.

D.T.'s

All week I've laboured on a villanelle.
I've mused and fretted and perspired,
But I've not been doing very well.

The rhymes are hard, the repeats are hell,
The whole scheme of things is rather tired.
All week I've laboured on a villanelle.

I've a list of words from zel to hydrogel,
But however I shuffle, it isn't inspired.
I've not been doing very well,

For constantly the words rebel,
They fidget and won't line up as required –
All week I've laboured on a villanelle.

Old D.T. (good name for a lover of Bells)
Could turn a mean villanelle – one to be admired,
But I've not been doing very well.

Clearly, it's a question of Hirondelle –
It must be whiskey that has the desired.
All week I've laboured on a villanelle
And I've not been doing very well.

Introducing the Revolutionary Oxford Free Verse

Designed for the ultimate reading experience,
   this poem can accelerate from 0-60 words in half a page.
And, as you'd expect, contains the very latest
   in poem technology.
Servo assisted metaphors.
Electronically controlled alliteration.
And shatter proof, heated rear images.
When you buy Oxford, you know you're getting quality,
   reliability and solid, cliché-proof construction.
Incorporating the latest aerodynamic forms,
   The Free Verse is built for the 21st century.
Gone are those days of riding bumpy metre.
No more cramped AABA membership.
No more couplets in dark lines.
With the new internal rhyme scheme,
   there's time to relax.
(The stereo rhythms are fitted as standard.)
Listen to the steady hum of the two letter assonance
   as you glide down the journey of your page.
With the modern dash – everything is clear.
Neatly typed.

And double spaced.

Check your enjoyment level at a glance.
Family?
There's room for the kids and teddy, too
   in our spacious stanzas.
So don't you get caught with enjambment.
Be informed.
Come and talk to us about The Oxford.
It's free.

Not a Kite

The dirty picture on the wall
is the cleanest thing in here.

The fat man sniffs, leans back in his chair
and points through the window.

Outside, the mud holds it all:
a stew of bolts, wire, grit, bits.

A mechanic beckons
an engine to the floor.

The fat man scratches, makes up a price.
'Six quid,' he says. 'Five for cash.'

I borrow a pen. The desk is gritty as a sump.
'Not a kite, is it?'

Outside, a man moves among the minis
looking for a decent door.

Issigonis Photographed

His office had the cut-away for draughtsmen.
A cartoon car driven through the sawmill.
Half spare tyre, half back seat,
engine sliced from rocker box to sump.

The tab washer was a mechanic's curse:
a sixpenny part and two days' labour
to take the engine out. Mini jokes:
lock the wheels, they get stolen for go-carts.

But Enzo Ferrari drove one and Princess Margaret.
Handbrake turns and driving sideways
in the Monte Carlo rally. The Italian Job
and headlights rolling round a Turin sewer.

It bounced a bit, a plodder on the straight,
but give it corners. My dad had a traveller.
I remember the indicator stalk
with green repeater bulb in the end.

The Bottom Back Nut

It's the sort of place you can't get
a half inch drive socket to, a knuckle
joint, a ten mill or a hammer. You can't
get round it because of the sump, you
can't reach it because you're not an orang-u-tan.

The sort where you're trying to
get, cursing at the speck in your
eyeball, when the neighbour says, cheerily
'having trouble?' The sort of place you
laugh off, wiping grease across your

cheek as you do so, where you break your
best screwdriver, smashing your knuckles against the
radiator's rusty back. It's that
place to get to properly, you need two
hundred quid's worth of tackle and

you could drop it off in twenty minutes. As it
is, in the road with a doubtful jack and wet
on your neck and your wife saying 'I'm
off now love,' it will take you three
hours and you still won't have done it.

Policemen Have Everything

Bicycle clips, capes, leather gloves
torches for looking up alleys and buildings

handcuffs and truncheons, notepads
radios to talk to each other

lights that flash, portable lights that flash
police aware signs, police slow signs, accident signs.

They have breathalysers and cones
boots and wellington boots. They have numbers.

They have clean cars that will easily
reach the speed limit. They have watches.

Apple

From the window, an angle of wing,
water and blur of buildings. Heat shiver of city.
The door opens like a bank vault: New York.

I stand and gaze. Like a President wave
to relatives. Size eights feel the heat.
This is entry into the U.S.A.

The rigmarole of luggage, law:
'Fruit forbidden. Verboten. Interdit.'
The eating of an apple.

The face on my passport is useful.
In the confusion of greetings
a hand dips my pocket and I am stolen.

At immigration, I must describe myself.
I am not yet here, a no-one,
my voice invisible against the ringing phone.

Africans Waving

Not just those I spoke to, enjoyed a meal with,
shared a joke and drank with, laughed and sang
and gave a present to; swapped stories and words,
shook and held hands and danced and loved with,

but those Africans waving, the children whistling
for our faces and giving a one, two handed wave
from their veranda. It catching like a smile
across the village, across the country.

William Agricola

It doesn't need words to say what he's feeling.
Just a look at his watery eyes and the twitch
in his cheekbone reminds me I'm leaving.

He keeps alive in conversation by the gentlest touch
on my arm. His fingers dance the letters A to Z for me
in subtle variation or a quick mime says it all.

My binoculars bring him new horizons
and he looks from one skyline to another,
compares what he sees with what he knows.

We sit until dusk when a tree frog starts,
its metallic clink hammering in the night
and I remember first hearing it.

The Lizard Man

'Quick! Quick! He's coming! The lizard man is coming!'
Sixty odd, in uniform, he walks up the hill,
seats himself, feet straight out, digs into both pockets:
'Here little man, here little man, ar-up, ar-up,'
and flings handfuls of sadza onto the rock.
'Wea, wea boy, little man, little man.'
His voice magics the lizard from his trance.

Unpeeling from his fixed place among the lichen,
movement says he's there. He jumps, spectacular orange,
from nowhere, from dust, from stone,
pushed out from a crevice by others behind.
'Look! Look!' Come green, come yellow and grey backs.
'Wea boy, wea boy, little man, little man.
Ar-up, ar-up. Wea, wea, wea, wea.'

The crowd he has conjured laugh:
laugh at the lizard in the lizard man's pocket,
laugh at the lizard in the lizard man's hair.
Empty, he gets up and goes down the hill,
his dark uniform visible for a long time.
They look back at red dust, deserted,
study the piled rocks, blink in African heat.

Zebra

We drive the road between them
and they kick and run into the Serengeti.

A few go with us for a while, then peel away,
leaving this one to dither in the tracks.

We hassle him to forty miles an hour
before he panics into new ground

to stand neck to tail making symmetry,
his lines distinct as fingerprints.

Our Bed is a Game Reserve

Elephant are dark circled by the trees
and you are pointing: a baby, protected by the herd,
hides in the swimming pool.
His mother has taken a fancy to my roses.
Through the window peers a giraffe.
He pulls leaves off the curtain, munches.
Buffalo graze at the bottom of the bed.

The way out is along the dust road
by the river which is the landing
which falls Victoria Falls to the lounge.
A jacaranda tree blooms purple in the garden
on the window-sill where the welcome home carnations
and lilies are. Smell of the bush: impala,
kudu cow at the water-hole, rhino.

A monkey on the garage roof peels a banana,
the upside-down crescent moon of Africa.
Lion squash on the duvet next to the cat
who doesn't see why he should share.
Bumi Hills is a postcard of the Great White Heron
carried through Huddersfield rain.
Aloes grow from behind my pillow.

On top of the wardrobe a leopard dozes,
his black mamba tail dangling.
A waiter called Never serves my message
on a silver tray: Duncan of England called.
He loves you so much. 'Where are you darling?
Why aren't you in this white room?'
An elephant trunk holds me to you.

Zimbabwe

Phoning Zimbabwe cost me five hundred pounds,
but I was in love and not missing Victoria Falls,
though I could have flown over it for the price
instead of your distant voice across two continents
crackling down a thinning phone line.

It's easy to be angry about this:
thinking as I clean my teeth late at night
after several glasses of wine: is it any wonder I left?
No contact between us stretching the point
like the distance of a continent between two phones.

Zimbabwe sounded wide as I listened to the weeks pass
and this romance enjoyed by the hotel guests,
thinning their figures in the African sun,
stretching themselves to pay for a safari to Bumi Hills
where the elephants push acacia leaves between their teeth.

Five hundred days and nights weren't enough
to clean out the romance and leave something to wonder at,
my anger crackling like an African leaf in African sun,
but thinning out finally to pay with boxes
in the back of my car and no phone ringing.

Ratatouille

Sometimes, whole days, weeks, months go by
and I do not say Yugoslavia.

There are other words: lozenge
cafeteria, vermouth, chemise.

Once, on a bridge, gaping into the water,
we both said enantiomorphic at the same time.

That was our hottest summer.
I can't remember the last time I said paso doble.

Fandango

From the white balcony, I study the bay,
watch a speedboat crossing the blue.
You hide in the bedroom from the heat of day.

The maid has fan-folded your negligée.
You invite me to see what cloth can do.
From the white balcony, I study the bay.

A speedboat is good at getting away.
I call you to watch its elegant skew.
You hide in the bedroom from the heat of day.

I want to be that boat, hurrying away
from the effort of land, rising at full screw
from the white balcony. I study the bay.

I'm boring myself with what I say.
How can you ever see my point of view?
You hide in the bedroom from the heat of day.

The boat leaves the water in disarray,
speeds out of sight to its rendezvous.
From the white balcony, I study the bay.
You hide in the bedroom from the heat of day.

Farewell (in the American Style)

We arrange to meet for lunch at the place
which now seems like ours. I am delayed
by traffic and already you are through
your first cup of coffee. I apologise
and shrug my coat, my camera into a vacant seat.

You nod, try a smile and put down your cup.
You are wearing your Mickey Mouse top
and your hair is held back with a clip.
We order. I shake out my serviette.
It is the kids, your husband, my letter.

Throughout the meal our talk moves
like the waitress over old ground,
until you surprise me with a cigarette.
I try to get a focus, but you wave me off
with the smoke, lean for an ashtray.

The bill arrives and I am quicker than you.
I have to go. I close my camera case
and leave you watching the cars.
It is the waitress, wiping, who calls:
'Have a nice day.'

End of the Ice Age

Skin barely admits
you're learning a new vocabulary:
the movement of lips.

The heat in your tongue is a risk.
You fear the sound of water in the valley,
the touch of wind on your legs, lips.

The buds push at their tips.
The tree roots loosen their hold on the hill,
beards of grass drip.

The thaw begins with your lips:
the stamen of your tongue reaching,
trying the taste of it.

To His

We could   or   if you'd prefer
or maybe just   .
It depends how you feel.
          , she says. I like to
especially with
but we don't have a   or
or even the   ,   ,   .
We could always   though,
but only if you
and promise not to   .
I promise, he says.
Let's   together then, she says
while we still have
and the
and a
to   with.

Lunch Box

In the big double bed of my lunch box,
I find the baby tomatoes, the slices of carrot
laid out ready, the doughnut with so much sugar
it makes the grapes sticky.

There is more here than any man could eat:
egg sandwich, pork pie, the sweet Harry gave me.
Others look envious, some comment
on the cucumber you have peeled.

When we argue, I worry about my lunch,
look in the fridge in the darkened kitchen
for the big double bed wonky on the wine,
the blur of plums against the plastic side.

Marriage is Buying a Car

Five thousand eight hundred and ninety nine pounds
very definitely only, you say, signing the cheque
with a new pen that makes your name
look like a signature from The Reader's Digest:

the one that comes in the letter saying:
'You have been selected, blah, blah,'
the one with the window envelope
containing the key to the brand new BMW,

the one that has the photograph
of Mr and Mrs Earnshaw from Somerset,
smiling with their two children and a quote about:
'how they very nearly didn't, blah, blah.'

All this and more as you weigh it briefly,
teasing the salesman. It is your biggest cheque ever
and we offer it a fanfare as he slips it in
the clear plastic wallet and into the drawer.

There are two keys and mine is the one
that's been burnt on the stove.
You've got the upholstery and the radio.
I've got the oily bits, the petrol and the driving.

Something You Can't Argue With

Like the push in your back
when the engines come on
and you know you've got them
to thrust you down the runway
and inescapably up,

like that only more so,
not in one place but all around,
filling the whole room,
not electric or storm,
but palpable, in the air,

a giant stirring, a spreading,
reaching like gravity,
magnetism, that bushy,
squashy feeling
like-poles produce,

a bounciness, invisible
yet there, pushing,
big, without question,
bigger than hurricane or volcano,
bigger than ocean, big.

Duncan Curry was born in 1957 and lives in Huddersfield. He gained a BA Honours degree at Bretton Hall College and an MA at the University of Lancaster. He teaches English at a local comprehensive school.

Smith/Doorstop Books

publish books, cassettes
and pamphlets by

Moniza Alvi
Simon Armitage
Sujata Bhatt
Liz Cashdan
Julia Casterton
Linda Chase
Debjani Chatterjee
Bob Cooper
Julia Copus
Tim Cumming
Duncan Curry
Peter Daniels
Carol Ann Duffy
Janet Fisher
Anna Fissler
Katherine Frost
John Harvey
Jo Haslam
Geoff Hattersley

Jeanette Hattersley
Keith Jafrate
John Lancaster
Peter Lane
John Lyons
Ian McMillan
Cheryl Martin
Eleanor Maxted
David Morley
Les Murray
Dorothy Nimmo
Pascale Petit
Eva Salzman
Lemn Sissay
Joan Jobe Smith
Martin Stannard
Mandy Sutter
Dennis Travis
Mary Woodward
Cliff Yates

For details of all our publications, and our current Competition, send an sae to The Poetry Business, The Studio, Byram Arcade, Westgate, Huddersfield HD1 1ND